INCREDIBLE ANIMAL LIFE CYCLES
LIFE CYCLE OF A KANGAROO

by Karen Latchana Kenney

pogo

Ideas for Parents and Teachers

Pogo Books let children practice reading informational text while introducing them to nonfiction features such as headings, labels, sidebars, maps, and diagrams, as well as a table of contents, glossary, and index.

Carefully leveled text with a strong photo match offers early fluent readers the support they need to succeed.

Before Reading

- "Walk" through the book and point out the various nonfiction features. Ask the student what purpose each feature serves.
- Look at the glossary together. Read and discuss the words.

Read the Book

- Have the child read the book independently.
- Invite him or her to list questions that arise from reading.

After Reading

- Discuss the child's questions. Talk about how he or she might find answers to those questions.
- Prompt the child to think more. Ask: Kangaroos are marsupials. What other animals are marsupials?

Pogo Books are published by Jump!
5357 Penn Avenue South
Minneapolis, MN 55419
www.jumplibrary.com

Library of Congress Cataloging-in-Publication Data

Names: Kenney, Karen Latchana, author.
Title: Life cycle of a kanagroo / by Karen Latchana Kenney.
Description: Minneapolis, MN : Jump!, 2018.
Series: Incredible animal life cycles
Series: Pogo books | Includes index.
Audience: Ages 7 to 10.
Identifiers: LCCN 2017057004 (print)
LCCN 2017056680 (ebook)
ISBN 9781624968174 (ebook)
ISBN 9781624968150 (hardcover : alk. paper)
ISBN 9781624968167 (pbk.)
Subjects: LCSH: Kangaroos—Life cycles—Juvenile literature.
Classification: LCC QL737.M35 (print)
LCC QL737.M35 K46 2018 (ebook) | DDC 599.2/22156—dc23
LC record available at https://lccn.loc.gov/2017057004

Editor: Jenna Trnka
Book Designer: Molly Ballanger

Photo Credits: Anan Kaewkhammul/Shutterstock, cover, 3; Bradley Blackburn/Shutterstock, 1, 23; Jean-Paul Ferrero/Pantheon/SuperStock, 4, 5, 18-19; Roland Seitre/Minden Pictures/SuperStock, 6-7; tap10/iStock, 8-9; Robin Smith/Getty, 10; SuDizzle/iStock, 11; Jak Wonderly/Getty, 12-13; John CancalosiPan/Pantheon/SuperStock, 14-15; SA Tourist/Shutterstock, 16; D. Parer & E. Parer-Cook/Minden Pictures/SuperStock, 17, 20-21.

Printed in the United States of America at Corporate Graphics in North Mankato, Minnesota.

TABLE OF CONTENTS

CHAPTER 1

A NEWBORN JOEY

A **newborn** kangaroo inches its way up its mother's body. It is just bigger than a jellybean. It cannot see. And it hasn't grown legs yet.

But this **joey** knows how to finds its mother's pouch. It pulls itself into the pouch with its tiny arms. This is part of the kangaroo's life cycle.

pouch

joey

The joey grows inside its mother's body for roughly one month. After it is born, it takes about three minutes to crawl and find the pouch.

Inside the pouch, the joey stays warm and safe. It drinks milk from its mother. The joey gets all the **nutrients** it needs to grow. Soon the little joey grows back legs and a tail.

After around five months, the joey sticks its head out. But it is not ready to leave the pouch.

DID YOU KNOW?

Kangaroos are **marsupials**. These **mammals** have pouches where their young grow. Wombats and opossums are two other kinds of marsupials.

CHAPTER 2

LEAVING THE POUCH

The joey stays in the pouch. It looks around while its mother hops and eats. It might nibble on some grass, too.

As the joey grows, the pouch gets crowded. The joey's legs can barely fit inside.

The joey first leaves the pouch by falling out. It tries to stand and hop. Its legs are wobbly. It stays close to its mother. Then it climbs back into the pouch.

DID YOU KNOW?

Only tree kangaroos can hop backward. Other kangaroos can only hop forward. And they cannot move their legs separately.

After a few more months,
the joey is ready for life
on land. It leaves the pouch.
But it still drinks its mother's
milk for a while longer.
It stays near her.

CHAPTER 3

FINDING A MOB

The joey grows bigger. It is now a **juvenile**. It learns from its mother. It follows her everywhere. She keeps the joey safe from danger.

Joeys also learn from each other. Males pretend to fight. They learn skills that will help them as adults.

In a year or more after it stops drinking its mother's milk, the juvenile is an adult. It finds a group to join. A group of kangaroos is called a **mob**.

TAKE A LOOK!

Each kangaroo goes through a life cycle. It has four **stages**:

newborn:
After one month or so of growing inside its mother, the tiny newborn crawls to the pouch.

young joey:
The young joey drinks milk and grows in the pouch for around nine months.

juvenile joey:
The joey leaves the pouch but stays close to its mother.

adult:
A year or more after it stops drinking its mother's milk, the joey becomes an adult.

Sometimes males in the mob fight. They stand up tall on their back feet. They grab each other with their front paws. Then one leans back on its tail. It uses its strong back legs to kick.

The winner will **mate** with a female. Soon a new baby joey will begin its journey. One day it will be an adult kangaroo.

DID YOU KNOW?

Kangaroo mobs live all over Australia and some nearby islands.

ACTIVITIES & TOOLS

HOPPING DISTANCE

Kangaroos are the only large mammals that hop. And they can jump far with their strong legs. Try this activity to see how far you can hop.

What You Need:
- measuring tape
- rocks
- paper
- pen
- calculator

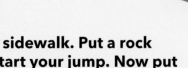

❶ Go outside on a driveway or sidewalk. Put a rock on the spot where you will start your jump. Now put a rock on the spot where you think you will land.

❷ Measure the distance from the starting to landing point. Write the measurement down.

❸ Now jump from the starting point. Put a rock down where you land.

❹ Measure the distance from the starting to landing point. Write down the number. Try jumping two more times. Measure the distances. Then use the biggest distance for the next step.

❺ Did you predict the right distance? If not, find the difference between the two measurements. Was it harder or easier than you thought it would be to jump a long distance?

GLOSSARY

joey: A young kangaroo.

juvenile: An older joey that is close to being an adult kangaroo.

mammals: Warm-blooded animals that have hair or fur and whose females make milk to feed their babies.

marsupials: A kind of mammal whose females have a pouch to carry their young.

mate: When a male and female animal come together to make babies.

mob: A group of kangaroos that lives together.

newborn: Something just recently born.

nutrients: Substances people, animals, and plants need to stay strong and healthy.

stages: Steps or periods of development.

INDEX

TO LEARN MORE

Learning more is as easy as 1, 2, 3.

1) Go to www.factsurfer.com

2) Enter "lifecycleofakangaroo" into the search box.

3) Click the "Surf" button to see a list of websites.

With factsurfer, finding more information is just a click away.